What they don't tell you about

ANGLO-SAXONS

MOOO!

By Bob Fowke

Dedicated to *Thrimilci*, the Saxon month when
cows were milked three times a day

Hodder
Children's

Hallo, my name's Ethelfrithelfroth, and if you can say that you can say anything. I'm a Saxon woman and I'm tough as a leather garter. Come with me and I'll show you all about the Anglo-Saxons. I hope you're tough too: this book is not for the faint-hearted ...

Text and illustrations, copyright © Bob Fowke 1998

The right of Bob Fowke to be identified as the author of the work has been asserted by him in accordance with the Copyright, Designs and Patents Act 1988.

Produced by Fowke & Co. for Hodder Children's Books

Cover image supplied by Mary Evans Picture Library

Published by Hodder Children's Books 1998

0340 709219

10 9 8 7 6 5 4 3

Hodder Children's Books
a Division of Hodder Headline plc
338 Euston Road
London NW1 3BH

Printed and bound by The Guernsey Press Co. Ltd., Guernsey, Channel Islands
A Catalogue record for this book is available from the British Library

CONTENTS

Watch out for the *Sign of the Foot*! Whenever you see this sign in the book it means there are some more details at the *FOOT* of the page. Like here.

SAXFAX

BEFORE WE BEGIN

There's a feast in the mead hall . It's been going on for months, although that's nothing special if you're a Saxon warrior. And it's been great - there's been boasting and drinking for breakfast, followed by drinking and boasting with a spot of poetry for lunch, and in the evenings there's been lots more drinking - and more boasting! After all, what's a warrior to do with his spare time?

All right, so there's been the odd fight. These lads have been feasting too long. It's time to head out on a proper war party ...

Mead is an alcoholic drink made from honey.

WHERE WILD WARRIORS WANDER

The Saxons were wild warriors from northern Europe who conquered what is now England in the years between AD 450 and 700. Early Saxons couldn't read or write so they didn't leave us any written records. We know very little about them - but we do know that fighting was what they liked doing best.

These wild warriors belonged to several barbarian nations or tribes and their homeland was in the area now covered by northern Holland and Germany, far beyond the reach of the civilized Roman Empire at that time. They're called *Anglo-Saxons* because their two largest nations were the Angles and the Saxons, but they're often just called *Saxons* for short.

 AD stands for *Anno Domini*, or 'Year of Our Lord', and means the number of years after the birth of Christ. This system of dating was introduced into Britain by the Anglo-Saxons.

Barbarian was a word used by the Romans to described uncivilized tribes. It comes from the Greek word for a foreigner.

The Anglo-Saxons believed that they were descended from a hero called *Sceaf* who had been washed up on a northern beach in an open boat in the dim and distant past. Boats were important to the Saxons. They lived near the sea and were expert sailors. In fact, there had been Saxon pirates in the North Sea for hundreds of years before they conquered Britain, so much so that the name *Saxon* was used as another word for 'pirate' among the poor old Romans who first suffered their attacks.

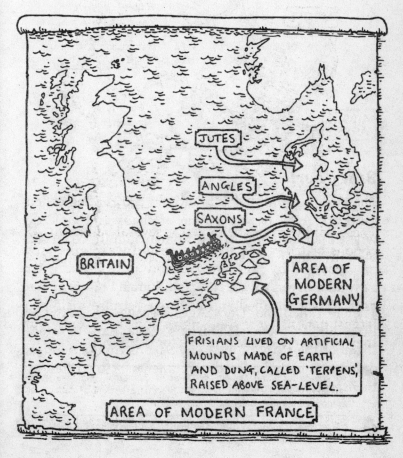

JUTES

ANGLES

SAXONS

BRITAIN

AREA OF MODERN GERMANY

FRISIANS LIVED ON ARTIFICIAL MOUNDS MADE OF EARTH AND DUNG, CALLED 'TERPENS', RAISED ABOVE SEA-LEVEL.

AREA OF MODERN FRANCE

YEAR BEER

Saxons often drank from *drinking horns*.

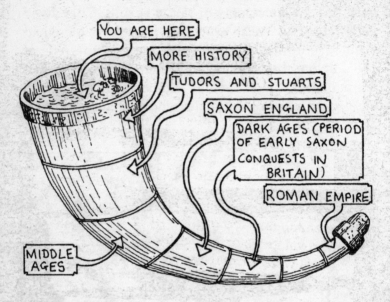

YOU ARE HERE

MORE HISTORY

TUDORS AND STUARTS

SAXON ENGLAND

DARK AGES (PERIOD OF EARLY SAXON CONQUESTS IN BRITAIN)

ROMAN EMPIRE

MIDDLE AGES

BLACK OUT!

The period from AD 400 to around 600 is often called the *Dark Ages*. It was a time of chaos and violence when the old world of the Roman Empire collapsed beneath a thousand barbarian attacks, including those of the early Saxons.

They're called the 'Dark Ages' because we know so little about them. Historians have had to piece together the story of the early Saxons from a handful of clues, mostly battered parchments written by their angry enemies.

Paper was unknown in Europe at that time. Everything was written on a sort of leather, called parchment.

Triads (no, not Chinese gangsters!) are very early Welsh or British poems.

Gildas was a British monk who wrote the *'Story of the Loss of Britain'* in AD 547.

Nennius, another British monk, wrote about Saxon attacks.

Saxon kings made *king lists* of their royal ancestors. Later these lists were written down.

The *Venerable Bede* was a Saxon monk who wrote a history of his people around AD 730.

The *Anglo-Saxon Chronicle* was started around AD 890 but refers back to earlier times.

Beowulf is a poem about Saxon heroes around the time of their conquest of Britain (see page 43).

MR AND MRS SAXON

The Roman writer Tacitus says the early Germans were large people with blue eyes and reddish or fair hair. This is probably what most of the early Anglo-Saxons looked like.

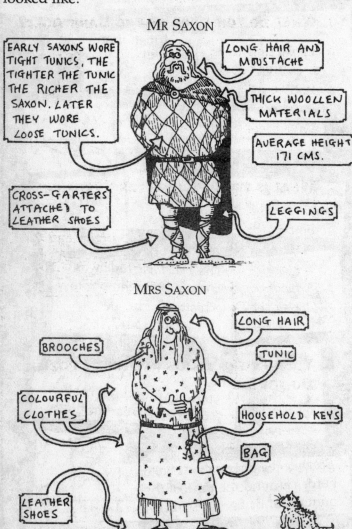

MR SAXON

EARLY SAXONS WORE TIGHT TUNICS, THE TIGHTER THE TUNIC THE RICHER THE SAXON. LATER THEY WORE LOOSE TUNICS.

LONG HAIR AND MOUSTACHE

THICK WOOLLEN MATERIALS

AVERAGE HEIGHT 171 CMS.

CROSS-GARTERS ATTACHED TO LEATHER SHOES

LEGGINGS

MRS SAXON

BROOCHES

LONG HAIR

TUNIC

COLOURFUL CLOTHES

HOUSEHOLD KEYS

BAG

LEATHER SHOES

ARE YOU IGNORANT?

*Check it out - are you the right type
to be a seriously savage Saxon?
Part 1*

1. WHAT DO YOU THINK OF THE DARK AGES?

a. Lovely time to be alive. Wish
   they could go on for ever
b. Horrible, why doesn't someone
   invent the electric light
c. Dark Ages? What's that?

2. WHAT IS THE ANGLO-SAXON CHRONICLE?

a. A costume drama series
   on television
b. A Saxon newspaper of
   the period
c. A record of events
   during the Saxon period

3. YOUR FRIEND STARTS RECITING A POEM. DO YOU?...

a. Tell him or her to shut up and
   stop being so sissy
b. Sit back and enjoy it
c. Listen and then tell him or
   her that you could do better

Answers on page 121

THE GOOD, THE BAD AND THE BARBARIC

The early Saxons were barbarians whose idea of a quiet night in was a drunken bone-fight in the mead hall. But over time the Saxons settled down and many later Saxons were saints and statesmen who helped to re-civilize Europe and end the barbaric Dark Ages.

Between them, the bad early Saxons and the good later Saxons made a huge impact on Britain. In AD 449, when the Saxons first arrived in force, people in Britain spoke a bit of Latin, and *Brythonic*, a language like Welsh. Two hundred years later most people in what is now *England* spoke an early form of *English*. They obeyed *English* laws and lived in *English* towns and villages.

You see, the early Saxons came as warriors, but they stayed on as settlers. As the years went by they either mingled with the locals or drove them out. The Angles were the largest group of settlers, so nearly everyone in what is now England came to call themselves Angles or *Aenglisc*  which is where the words *English* and *England* come from.

 Lots of Saxon names start with 'ae'. The two letters together are pronounced a bit like the 'a' in 'add'. So Aenglisc is pronounced 'Anglisc'.

ROMAN REMAINS

BRITAIN BEFORE THE SAXONS

Britain at the time of the Saxon invasions was full of British people, believe it or not. The British were Celts and the language they spoke, Brythonic, was a Celtic language , whereas the Saxons were Germans and Saxon was a German language.

THE STORY SO FAR

AD 43 The Romans invade Britain. The British Celts fight back bravely, but their war-chariots are no match for the Roman armies. The British living in the area of modern England and Wales are defeated and all of Britain, except Scotland, becomes a province of the Roman Empire.

AD 43-280 The British become civilized members of the Roman Empire. They have roads and cities. The rich live in comfortable houses, and most people learn to speak Latin, the Roman language, as well as Brythonic. They are often called Romano-Britons.

 Celts, or Celtic speaking people, once lived in much of northern and western Europe. Those that lived in England were mainly tall with fair hair. Those in Wales, Ireland and Scotland were mainly smaller with dark hair.

AD 280 Saxon pirate attacks cause serious problems. The Romans build a number of massive forts along the coast, known as the *Forts of the Saxon Shore*.

AD 360 The first collapse: barbaric Picts from Scotland, Scots from Ireland and Saxons overrun Britain. Chaos reigns for two years.

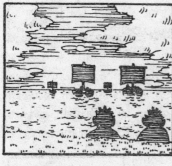

AD 409 The Roman army is withdrawn from Britain to fight other barbarians on mainland Europe. The British must defend themselves against barbarian attack.

AD 449 Saxon warriors, who have been invited into Britain to help defend the Romano-British against the Scots, turn on their British guests - the Saxon conquests have begun.

The word *Pict* comes from the Latin for 'painted'. They were northern Celts and probably decorated themselves with a blue dye called woad.

The *Scots* came from Ireland originally. Until around AD 1400 the word 'Scot' meant an Irishman.

SOFT CITIES

How would you feel if your town was attacked by a pack of barbarians armed with swords and spears? Pretty upset probably. That's how the Britons must have felt in AD 450. For four hundred years Britain had been ruled by Rome. They had cities, roads, town halls, public baths and libraries, and they even had central heating. They were civilized. They didn't want to be bothered with war and fighting - but Saxons did!

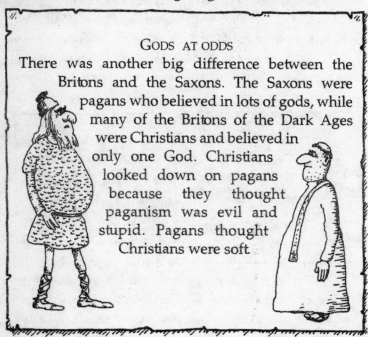

GODS AT ODDS

There was another big difference between the Britons and the Saxons. The Saxons were pagans who believed in lots of gods, while many of the Britons of the Dark Ages were Christians and believed in only one God. Christians looked down on pagans because they thought paganism was evil and stupid. Pagans thought Christians were soft.

SWORDS FOR SALE

Saxons and other barbarians liked fighting. They also liked money. So, for hundreds of years the Romans paid barbarians to fight *for* them instead of *against* them. On the borders of the Roman Empire there were often Saxon soldiers fighting alongside the regular

Roman army. Saxons like this were probably living in Yorkshire before AD 400. It worked fine as long as the Romans were strong enough to control them - but what would happen if the Saxons turned against their employers?

In AD 449 the Britons were about to find out ...

SAX ATTAX!

WE'VE COME TO STAY

HOW IT ALL BEGAN

The Roman province of Britain was alone like a lost duckling without its mother duck after the Roman army left Britain around AD 409. The Romano-Britons struggled on alone, but all kinds of barbarians hovered greedily beyond the borders, ready to pounce.

Forty years later barbarian attacks were getting out of hand. It seems that a British leader named Vortigern, the 'Proud Tyrant', asked a band of Saxon warriors to fight for him against the barbarian Scots. These Saxon warriors came in three or more ships and landed at a place called *Ypines Fleot* in Kent . Their leaders were two tough killers called Hengist and Horsa. Many more warriors soon joined them.

The name of the county of Kent comes from the British tribe which used to live there, the Cantii.

18

Just six years after they arrived, Hengist and Horsa quarrelled with Vortigern, perhaps because he hadn't paid them. There was a battle, the first of many such battles. Horsa was killed but the Saxons won. Then in 457, at a place called *Crecgan Ford*, also somewhere in Kent, four thousand Britons were killed. The remainder of the British army fled before the Saxons 'like fire' until they reached the safety of London. The first Saxon kingdom in Britain had been born.

Other Saxon chiefs were quick to follow the example of Hengist and Horsa. In 477 the founders of the kingdom of the South Saxons, or Sussex as we call it today, landed in three ships, killed many Britons and drove others into a wood near the Roman fort of Anderida - modern Pevensey. In 491 the Saxons besieged the fort itself and killed all the Britons inside it. The Britons were battered by Saxon attacks all along the south and east coasts.

LET'S GO BOATING

Saxon ships were large open rowing boats. About thirty warriors manned the oars and a typical war party was made up of three boats and about a hundred men As well as riding the ocean waves, they could be rowed in shallow waters, ideal for inland attacks up rivers or for landing on deserted beaches late at night.

 The numbers of warriors in most battles were usually very small in the Dark Ages. One Saxon law describes a gang of seven men as 'thieves', seven to thirty-five as a 'band' and just thirty-six as a *'here'*, meaning a host or army.

 The keel is a plank which juts down beneath the ship to stop it rolling from side to side.

WHAT A BOAR!

The warriors who scrambled to shore from their shallow boats were well armed.

A RICH MAN MIGHT HAVE A HELMET MOUNTED WITH THE SAXON 'BOAR-CREST' PERHAPS COVERED IN GOLD

ASH-SHAFTED SPEAR, UP TO 2 METRES LONG.

FOR CHOICE, A HUGE SWINGING AXE AND A FRANSISCA, OR THROWING AXE

ROUND WOODEN SHIELD, COVERED IN LEATHER

IRON SHIELD BOSS

SCRAMASAXE, A LONG DEADLY KNIFE

SWORD, ABOUT A METRE LONG

Swords were very precious. Ordinary warriors couldn't afford them. They were handed down from one generation to the next and carefully looked after. In the tenth century, the Saxon Prince Athelstan gave a sword to his brother which had been owned three hundred years earlier by a famous king called Offa (more on him on page 105).

Early German warriors fought naked or wearing only short cloaks, but by Saxon times the rich noblemen wore iron mail shirts. Later still the mail was sewn into a garment like knee-length combinations with wide leg holes so that it could be put on over the head.

CHARGE!

A Saxon war-party on the rampage must have been a terrifying sight. Early German warriors are described by the Roman writer Tacitus as holding their shields in front of their mouths and giving out a harsh roar. As they fought they chanted praises to Thunor, the god of thunder.

ROAR!!

Battles tended to be a scrum of fights between individual soldiers. Expert warriors were respected in the same way as famous sportsmen are today. Here's a later description of a fight of one against two, from

'The Lives of the Two Offas' written in St Albans. Two men have attacked the handsome young Offa:

> *With one stroke of his sword he struck down one of them, slashing off the crest of his helmet and piercing the skull to the brain, and casting him down as the death-rattle sounded. Then he rapidly pursued the other ... prostrating him with a lethal wound.*

STANDARD

During the battle the warriors might plant a standard in the ground. On the tip of the standard would be the figure of a fierce animal, often a boar or a stag. Around the standard they might form the Saxon *scildburgh* or 'shield wall'. To make a shield wall the warriors formed a line or a circle with their shields touching each other and awaited the advance of their enemies.

The early Saxons showed no mercy to their victims. Women and children were often slaughtered during their raids. Later the British monk Adomnan suggested a 'Law of the Innocents' to protect women and children. British kings accepted this law - but the Saxons didn't.

The British and the Saxons disagreed about a lot of things.

SOLDIER, SOLDIER

*Check it out - are you the right type
to be a seriously savage Saxon?
Part 2*

1. IT'S YOUR BIRTHDAY. WHICH PRESENT WOULD YOU LIKE BEST?

a. A sword
b. A huge swinging axe
c. A toy soldier called Egfrith

2. SOMEONE HAS CHALLENGED YOU TO A FIGHT IN THE PLAYGROUND. DO YOU?..

a. Go home early complaining
   of a headache
b. Silently prepare for battle
c. Charge at him or her with
   a harsh roar

3. WHAT IS A SHIELD BOSS?

a. The leader of a war party
b. The iron centre of a shield
c. The metal rim of a shield

Answers on page 121

24

WHAT IS THE MEANING OF BIRMINGHAM?

If all the Saxons had been warriors they would not have changed the world as much as they did. But they weren't. Thousands upon thousands of Saxon settlers followed the warriors. They changed the face of Britain for good. We know where many of them settled from place names. Does where you live end in 'ton, 'ham, or 'ing?

Ingas meant a group of followers. So *Haestingas*, or *Hastings* as we call it today, is where the family and followers of *Haesta* settled. Likewise *Reading* is where the followers of *Reada* started to farm.

Tun meant a village, so if your village ends in 'ton as in *Drayton*, you too live in an early Saxon settlement.

Ham meant home. Places ending in 'ham such as *Swaffham* were also started by the Saxons.

Now you can work out the meaning of *Birmingham*!

Birmingham means 'Beornmund's people's home'. The Beornmund bit was shortened to 'Birm'. Wonder what Birm would have made of that?

Mixed messages

The Saxons were ruthless warriors, but it's wrong to think that they drove all the British out of England. More likely, a lot of British people stayed on under their new rulers. Many would have had no choice, having been enslaved. The Saxon word for the British, *wahl* or *welisc* meaning 'foreigner' , was also used to mean a slave.

But it wasn't all fighting. There must have been a lot of mixing between the two cultures. To start with, it seems that the Saxons often settled on unfarmed land between the old Roman villa estates, which were probably still being farmed by the British. In other places British and Saxon farmers lived side by side in the same villages.

Very early on it seems that there were marriages between Saxon and British men and women. For instance, *Cerdic*, the war chief who founded Wessex, the Kingdom of the West Saxons, was first in the line

Welisc is where the word *Welsh* comes from. The British didn't call themselves Welsh. They called themselves the *Cymry*, meaning 'companions'.

of kings from which all later English kings are descended. His name is Celtic so he probably had a British mother. Likewise one of the earliest kings of Lindsey, a Saxon kingdom in Lincolnshire, was called Caedbad which is based on the Celtic word *cad* meaning a battle.

We know that Saxons and British Celts living in England both tended to be large with fair hair. Within a few generations, once they were all speaking English, it was impossible to tell one from the other.

CELTIC COUNTERATTAX!

THE BRITISH FIGHT BACK

BUT FIRST – THE SAXONS SPREAD OUT

There was a lot more fighting than mixing to begin with. In the fifty years from 450-500 many Saxon armies savagely attacked lands controlled by the British.

AD 495 Cerdic, founder of Wessex, the kingdom of the West Saxons, lands near Southampton with five ships. In a few years he conquers a large kingdom in the south of England.

By AD 500 Angles have landed in the east of Britain, founding the kingdom which will become known as East Anglia and making their way north of London into the southern Midlands.

By AD 500 Saxon pirates set up pirate bases along the north east coast. Later this region will become Northumbria, one of the most powerful Saxon kingdoms.

By AD 500 many Britons have fled across the English Channel. They form a new kingdom in what is now the French region of Brittany.

BRITISH BLOBS

When the Roman bishop Germanus visited Kent in 447, the leaders of the British still dressed like Roman nobles. They were *'brilliant in dress and surrounded by a fawning multitude'*. Just fifty years later Roman civilization had all but disappeared under pressure from Saxon attacks. The British kingdoms were ruled by warrior kings who behaved very like Saxon kings.

It was tough for the Britons. Their old Romano-British civilized way of life was under threat from all sides. But odd blobs of civilized Romano-British life lingered on in parts of Britain.

- The Roman fountains kept on flowing in Carlisle until at least 670.

- There was still a small British kingdom called Elmet in Yorkshire around 620.

- But the main British blobs were on the edges of England:

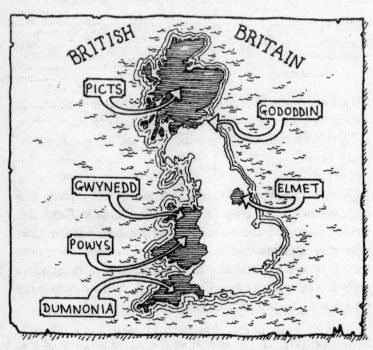

It was from these kingdoms that the fight back against the Saxons was launched ...

Of all the leaders of the Britons, the most mysterious is 'King Arthur'. The only certain thing about him is that, if he did exist, he was nothing like the King Arthur of story books!

In 450, when Vortigern, the 'proud tyrant', made the big mistake of inviting Hengist and Horsa to Kent, the British seem to have been divided into two parties. One side *may have been* led by Vortigern. The other side *may have been* led by 'the last of the Romans', a nobleman called Ambrosius Aurelianus. And Arthur *may have been* a war leader for Ambrosius' party.

But although Arthur is lost in the darkest days of the Dark Ages, he is mentioned in a few scraps of early parchments ...

'HE WAS NO ARTHUR'

In 593, after a year of feasting, a band of brave British warriors set out from the hall of Din Eidyn (modern Edinburgh) in the British Kingdom of the Gododdin in southern Scotland. Their tragic story is told in a long, sad poem 'Y Gododdin' by the British poet Aneirin. Aneirin himself rode with the heroes on their 'rough-maned horses like swans'.

The warriors' mission was to attack the stronghold of Catterick which had been captured by a brutal Saxon king called Aethelfrith the Ferocious. The raid was a disaster and most of the British warriors were killed.

But the really interesting thing about this poem is that it says of the leader of the British band that 'he was no Arthur', meaning he wasn't a very good leader. This is the first ever mention of King Arthur and shows that people of that time knew that he was a famous British war leader.

Not every one thought Arthur was a hero. Other British poems are quite rude about him:

The Three Wicked Uncoverings blames Arthur for the conquest of the British by the Saxons, because he took the head of the pagan Celtic god Bran from Tower Hill in London. Bran was meant to protect the British against foreign invasion. Perhaps this poem was written by a Briton who was still a pagan.

The Three Red Ravagers describes Arthur as a curse on Britain and a bit stupid.

SAXONS SLAUGHTERED SHOCK!

It's unlikely that Arthur was stupid. Nennius the Welsh monk tells us that Arthur was a war leader who fought twelve victorious battles against the Saxons. The first was in Lincolnshire, several were in Scotland, one was near Chester, and the last and most important was at a place called 'Mount Badon', which was probably near Bath. In this battle, which must have taken place around AD 500, *'there fell in one onslaught of Arthur's 960 men and none slew them but he alone'*.

After the Battle of Mount Badon the Saxons had to run for it. Many left for the mainland of Europe where they were given land by a German king. The German region of Saxony may be named after them.

And the Britons settled down to enjoy years of peace and plenty ...

BUT NOT FOR EVER!

CRAZY KINGDOMS

KINGS AND THEIR COMPANIONS

WE'RE BACK!

Peace and Saxons went together like custard and cabbage. By AD 550 Saxons were back on the warpath all over England. Britain was in for more than two hundred years of warfare.

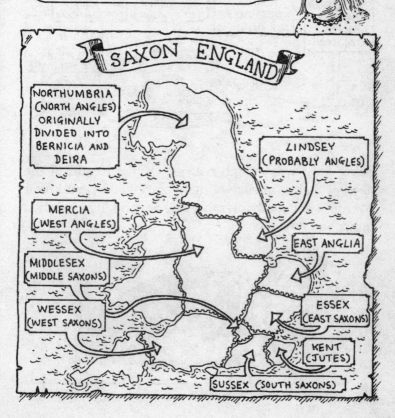

SAXON ENGLAND

NORTHUMBRIA (NORTH ANGLES) ORIGINALLY DIVIDED INTO BERNICIA AND DEIRA

LINDSEY (PROBABLY ANGLES)

MERCIA (WEST ANGLES)

EAST ANGLIA

MIDDLESEX (MIDDLE SAXONS)

WESSEX (WEST SAXONS)

ESSEX (EAST SAXONS)

KENT (JUTES)

SUSSEX (SOUTH SAXONS)

The king thing

Kings were top of the Saxon heap. It was Saxons who first introduced coronations to England. But not all kings were equal: little kings were subject to bigger kings, and usually one extra-powerful king made himself *Bretwalda* or 'Britain ruler' and was top king of everybody and his kingdom became the top kingdom. Under-kings had to fight for their masters if called upon.

KINGDOM THING

Being king was a high-risk job. Kings fought at the head of their armies. Not many survived beyond their twenties, and probably only one Saxon king ever died in his bed .

 Oswy, king of Northumbria 642-71.

Kings did not inherit their crowns from their fathers. Saxons chose their kings either for life or simply to lead them during a particular war. One way of counting the votes was by a *wapentake*. The warriors held

up their weapons and the weapons were counted. The German Franks used to lift up the new king on his shield to show their choice, and perhaps the ancient Saxons did the same.

Any male member of the royal family could be chosen; it was a case of the best man for the job. The one thing he had to have was royal blood. In fact royal blood wasn't enough. To be a king you had to prove that you were descended from a god! All except one of the Saxon royal families claimed to be descended from the god *Woden* at a time before they came to England 🐾 .

THE ORIGIN OF THE KINGS OF NORTHUMBRIA
Woden begot Beldeg, begot Beornec 🐾
begot Gechbrond, begot Aluson,
and so on ...

East Saxon kings claimed descent from the German god Saxnot, the 'Sword Bearer'.

Means: Woden was the father of Beldeg, who was the father of Beornec etc.

Saxon kings could get stinking rich with wealth looted from the British, and wealth given as tribute by lesser chiefs and kings.

They showed off their wealth with precious objects. Saxon craftsmen were very skilful. The greatest hoard of Saxon treasure ever found was excavated in 1938-9 from a field at *Sutton Hoo* in Suffolk. The treasure was buried inside a ship which was then covered in earth. There was no body, and the burial is thought to be a monument to Raedwald, king of the East Angles and Bretwalda of southern England around AD 600 who may have died at sea or abroad.

The Sutton Hoo treasures include gold and silver jewellery, a sword, a harp, a Roman dish, armour and a helmet.

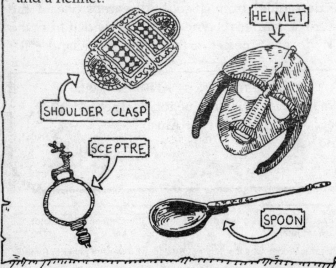

SHOULDER CLASP

HELMET

SCEPTRE

SPOON

FEELING COMPANIONABLE?

Every German king, including Saxon kings, lived with a group of faithful 'companions' called *thegns* or *gesith*. These were young warriors of noble blood. They lived in the king's hall, feasted with him and fought beside him. The Roman writer Tacitus says that, when not fighting, companions did nothing except drink and enjoy themselves. They were too lazy even to hunt. Kings were often known as 'ring-givers'. They had to win battles and to give their companions expensive presents in order to keep their support.

The worst thing a companion could do was to leave a battle alive after his king had been killed. As one Saxon poet  put it:

> *Our spirits shall be sterner, hearts the keener*
> *Courage the greater, as our strength fades.*
> *Here on the ground lies our lord, a good man cut down.*
> *The man who thinks of leaving the battle now will regret it for ever.*

Pronounced *thayns*.

His poem is called *The Battle of Maldon*. It describes a battle which a band of Saxons lost to Vikings in the tenth century.

39

TALL HALLS

All the feasting and fun took place in the lord or king's hall. To this day the big house in many villages is called the 'hall'.

CENTRAL COLUMNS, PERHAPS COVERED IN GOLD OR SILVER

HOLE IN ROOF FOR SMOKE

PERHAPS ANTLERS OR STAGS' HEADS

TAPESTRIES

LORD OR KING (CHIEF GUEST SAT OPPOSITE)

SOUP OF THE DAY

DOGS

CENTRAL FIRE

Most halls were single-storey like barns with smaller outhouses grouped round, but later some had two stories. They weren't always safe. In 978, *'the entire witan [a gathering of the nation's top nobles] fell from an upper chamber at Calne, except the holy Archbishop Dunstan who supported himself upon a beam'*.

THATCHED ROOF

WOODEN BEAMS

COMPANIONS – SEATED IN ORDER OF IMPORTANCE

SHIELDS AND WEAPONS

WOMEN SAT ON THE CROSS-BENCHES

OIL LAMPS

DRUNK AS A SKUNK IN A BUNK

Drinking horns don't stand up on their own. Once filled, the contents have to be drunk before the horn can be put down. This led to much drunkenness. During a feast warriors would stagger to their feet and make boasts about how brave they were or swear wild oaths of loyalty to their chief before slumping back for another swig from the drinking horn. Saxon writing is full of descriptions of men collapsing and dying through too much drink. In their drunkenness the 'champions' got rougher and rougher. Gales of drunken laughter would shake the roof beams. Bones and other objects might be thrown at fellow drinkers. Drinking bouts often ended in violence.

When the fire burned low and the men could drink no more, the benches were cleared and the floor was set out with beds or bolsters. Above or beside each man's sleeping place were set his shields and weapons. They were always ready for war.

TIME FOR A TUNE

While the companions were still half sober they might listen to a poet telling heroic tales of their people or singing the praises of the chief or king. Early Saxons couldn't read or write and the poets spoke from memory, often to the sound of a harp. In later years one of these poems was written down ...

BEOWULF

Beowulf is one of the oldest poems written in English. It tells the story of a hero, Beowulf, of the Swedish tribe of the Geats, who sailed to Denmark to the hall of a Danish king.

A man-eating monster called Grendel had caused trouble, carrying off the king's companions at night while they slept and then eating them: 'By morning all the bench-boards would be drenched with blood' as the poet puts it. While staying in the hall, Beowulf wrestled with Grendel and pulled off one of its arms so that the monster died in agony.

SHGLOOF

But that's not the end of the story. Grendel's mum came along to get her own back. Beowulf had to kill Mum as well, tracking her to her underwater cave. 'The sword took her hard on the neck and broke the rings of bone; the broad sword passed straight through her death-doomed flesh. She fell to the floor. The sword was gory,' says the poet.

KING THING - AGAIN

One of these things has been chosen to be king. Which one is it?

Answer The one on the shield

A FEW THINGS TO DO WITHOUT DRINKING

The companions did have a few other activities apart from drinking, boasting and fighting.

Gambling: Germans, including early Saxons, were so fond of gambling that men would even bet themselves on a throw of the dice, becoming slaves if they lost.

PLACE YOUR BETS

I AM MY BET!

Caroles: the Saxons and the British both liked caroles, which were a mixture of singing and dancing.

But there's no doubt that singing, dancing, gambling, and even drinking, came a very poor second to fighting as the companions' favourite activity. After all that's what the king needed them for.

FIVE PENCE PER FINGER!

PAW LAWS ...

PRICE OF POWER

Among Saxons, the more important you were, the higher your price or *wergild* . Wergild was the money that had to be paid to a victim's family if you killed or wronged him or her in some way. The wergild for a nobleman was much higher than for a *churl*, or free peasant. Slaves had no wergild at all, although if you killed one you still had to pay his or her owner the price of about eight oxen.

WESSEX WERGILD

SLAVES – NOTHING WORTH SPEAKING OF

CHURLS OR CEORLS (FREE PEASANTS) – 200 SHILLINGS

NOBLE WARRIOR COMPANIONS, CALLED THEGNS OR GESITH – 600 SHILLINGS

KING OR CHIEF – THE SKY'S THE LIMIT!

Wergild means 'man-price'.

The highest wergilds were paid out for murder, but there were plenty of other crimes carefully spelled out in the laws of different Saxon kings. You might pay five pence for the finger of a churl and twenty pence for the finger of a thegn. Here are the payments which would be due to a churl's family in Wessex under King Alfred the Great:

Thegns were noble, churls were commoners - but not too common. In the early days a churl could hope to become a thegn: it all depended on land. A *hide* of land was enough to support one family. If a churl could get his hands on at least five hides, he could become a thegn. Later the thegns grew more powerful and they made the churls work for them. It became almost impossible to move from one class to another.

A shilling was worth twelve old pence. It was in use until 1971 when it was abolished. In Saxon times a shilling was worth a lot.

WEIGH YOUR WORDS!

Under the laws of King Alfred, if you could persuade 'twelve king's thegns' to swear that you were innocent of murder - then you were innocent! Oaths were all you needed. You could do the same with churls, but you would need more of them, because just as different classes had different wergilds, so they also had different 'strengths' of oath. The oath of a thegn counted for more than the oath of a churl.

Gradually a system of law courts grew up, based on *hundreds*, which were areas of land often the size of a *hundred* hides. Hundred courts met in the open air about once a month. All churls took part in their local court.

The meeting place for a hundred court was called a moot.

Ow!

If no one would swear for you, you might choose to rely on God to prove your innocence. 'Trial by ordeal' was a painful way of asking God for his opinion. It was especially popular once the Saxons became Christian (more on that later). Here's one form of ordeal - but don't try this at home if you know what's good for you!

1. Plunge your hand into a cauldron of boiling water up to the wrist or elbow and pick up a stone from the bottom.

2. Carry the stone 2.7 metres.

3. Bandage your hand.

4. Three days later unwrap the bandage. If your damaged hand is not infected, then you're innocent. God has proved it by helping to heal you.

DUEL!

Another way for God to settle a case was by·a duel, or 'trial by combat'. The idea was that God would help the person who was in the right. Women and old people could choose a champion to fight for them. Duellists took it in turn to strike each other and the idea was to strike a few very powerful blows. Before any duel there was always a long argument over who should strike first. It could make a big difference, although not always. Take this description of a duellist's blow during a fight between two champions called Agnarus and Biarco:

Agnarus cut through the front of the helmet, wounded the skin of the scalp and had to let go of his sword which became locked in the vizor holes ... then Biarco passed his fine-edged blade through the midst of Agnarus' body. Agnarus, in supreme suppression of his pain gave up the ghost with his lips relaxed into a smile.

MMMPHFF!

PAINFUL PUNISHMENTS

Imagine you've been found guilty and now it's time for punishment. You can't afford to pay any wergild and you'll just have to suffer. There's no proper prison because there are no stone buildings worth speaking of - unless you count being shut up in a shed with your hands and feet tied up while you wait for trial.

Cutting off of upper lip (other bits could also be cut off, such as hands, nose, ears, or tongue).

Scalping

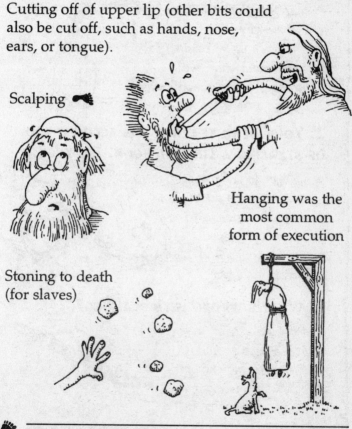

Hanging was the most common form of execution

Stoning to death (for slaves)

First used by the Saxons, as far as is known. Later, in the seventeenth century, English soldiers were paid £5 per head for dead Irish rebels. Heads were heavy so they took *scalps* instead. When English soldiers were sent to America, native Americans learned scalping from them.

IT'S THE LAW!

*Check it out - are you the right type
to be a seriously savage Saxon?
Part 3*

1. WHAT IS A WERGILD?

a. A trade union that only
   meets by moonlight
b. A type of wolf
c. The price to be paid to
   someone if you have
   wronged them in some way

2. YOUR HEAD TEACHER HAS ACCUSED YOU OF STEALING A LIBRARY BOOK. DO YOU?..

a. Challenge the head
   teacher to a duel
b. Ask your friends to
   speak up for you
c. Start crying and
   say it isn't fair

3. WHAT'S WRONG WITH SCALPING?

a. Nothing at all
b. It's a savage and
   barbaric punishment
c. It's a bit messy and
   the knife gets blunt

Answers on page 121

CALL OUT THE SHERIFF!

There were no policemen in Saxon times. In fact there was so little law and order that one law ordered all travellers to carry horns to blow if ever they wandered off the beaten track - to warn people that they were coming so as to show that they weren't thieves!

There were no policemen, but there were *sheriffs*. English counties, or *shires*, were started by the Saxons and the king's official in each shire came to be called a *reeve*. Put the two together and you get *shire-reeve*, or 'sheriff'. The sheriff was a major figure in the shire court, which tried cases which were too important for the hundreds courts. The sheriff was important, but the local *ealdorman*, later known as an 'earl' was even more important. *Ealdormen* were nobles who controlled the shires.

POWER TOWER

WITAN, OR GRAND COUNCIL, TO ADVISE THE KING, MADE UP OF THEGNS, EALDORMEN AND LATER, BISHOPS

KING

SHIRES - CONTROLLED BY SHERIFFS AND EALDORMEN

HUNDREDS - MADE UP OF A HUNDRED HIDES

HIDES - FARMED BY CHURLS

Churls were the foundation blocks of Saxon society. As long as the churls kept farming their hides of land, the tower would not topple over ...

DOWN ON THE FARM

LIFE IN THE MUD

FROWNS FOR TOWNS

Early Saxons frowned on towns. Towns were for softies like the Romano-Britons. According to Tacitus, the Germans, which included the Saxons, couldn't even bear houses built in rows: *'they live apart, each by himself, as woodside, plain, or fresh spring attracts him'*.

Most of the warriors and their families who came to Britain built their first grubby huts in the countryside. Only a few set up camp among the stone ruins of the cities, ruins which some Saxons thought were the work of giants.

Some settlers set up house on their own: do you live in a place ending in wic or wick, such as Stanwick? *Wic* is Saxon for a farm or enclosure.

There was a whole range of house types available for the newly arrived settler to choose for the design of his building:

small pit-huts, often used as storage sheds

larger pit-huts used as houses

small halls with plank walls

great hall for chiefs

STRIP OFF AND START WORK

Having built their houses, they set out to farm the land, using the 'open field' system. Open fields were not fields with the gate left open; they were two or three huge fields farmed by all the people of a village. The fields were divided into narrow *strips* and each family received a number of strips to farm. Every year one field was left *fallow* - without crops growing on it - so that the soil could recover its fertility.

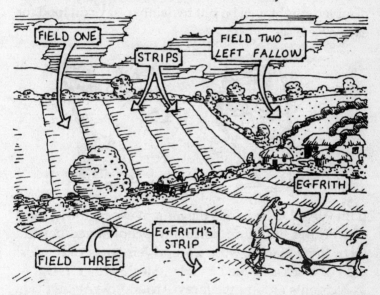

FIELD ONE

STRIPS

FIELD TWO – LEFT FALLOW

EGFRITH

EGFRITH'S STRIP

FIELD THREE

The life of a churl was hard, and got harder, even if he had a slave or two to help him . In early Saxon times his duty was to give food-rent direct to the king and to fight for him in battle. In later years, as the thegns grew more powerful, churls paid tribute to their local lords in the form of labour. A *cottar* for instance was a poor peasant who worked for his lord

Slaves cost roughly twice as much as horses.

each Monday and three days a week at harvest time - which left three days per week to harvest his own strips. When the Saxons became Christians, a cottar working on Sunday could be fined sixty shillings. If he couldn't pay it he might be made into a slave. Life was definitely better in the early days.

ELF TROUBLE

Most Saxons didn't live very long. The sick and the disabled might well be put to death to save on food for everyone else.

If they lived to be adults they might expect thirty years of working life, since not many people lived beyond forty (they started work around ten years old). Most died of disease or died a violent death either in war or in accidents around the farm. Around twenty per cent of Saxons suffered from broken bones.

Saxons believed in elves. They thought that illness was caused by evil elves who shot darts into their victims. The elves had to be driven out, which makes some of their ideas for treatment seem pretty basic:

> 'if a horse is elf-shot, whatever elf is involved this will cure him ... take a stick, strike him on the back.'

Working on the same principle, people with mental problems were beaten and cattle were driven through smoke to drive out evil.

Not all cures were so unpleasant. Bathing was meant to be good for health, although it wasn't something that Saxons liked to do too much of. They made steam baths by pouring water on to hot stones, or they could *sleep next to a fat child* as a way of keeping warm.

FOOD FOR THOUGHT

The main crops were wheat, rye, barley, beans and oats. Saxons slopped these down as porridge, cakes, bread and other simple foods. There was also meat, much of it slaughtered in autumn and then preserved by salting, thus saving on winter fodder. They even ate horse meat, although this was banned after 787. By that time the Saxons had become Christian and eating horse meat was thought to be a pagan custom.

There were other special laws about what you could eat. How about this law of King Edgar:

'if a hen drink human blood, it is lawful to eat it after three months.' Meaning it was forbidden to eat the hen for three months after it drank the blood.

Hens that drank human blood - where did they find the blood?! Does it make you wonder what life was really like down on the farm?

A RUMBLE WITH THE THUNDER GOD

YOU MAY BE MORE OF A PAGAN THAN YOU THOUGHT!

IT'S A DEAD CERTAINTY

Pagan Saxons did not fear death - or at least they tried not to show they did. They believed that the moment of their death was decided by three 'fates' before they were born. The fates were three women - representing the past, present and future - who lived beneath the great circle of the Earth.

YOU CAN HAVE A WONDERFUL LIFE WITH LOTS OF MONEY AND LIVE TO A HUNDRED.

YOU CAN HAVE A HORRIBLE, MISERABLE LIFE AND DIE BEFORE YOU'RE TWENTY.

WAY OUT

HUMAN SOULS

Since the time of a Saxon's death was already decided, there was no point in worrying about it. *'Fearlessness is better than a faint heart for any man who puts his nose out of doors. The length of my life and the day of my death were fated long ago'* as one poet put it.

Warriors especially needed to be brave - Woden was waiting for them.

WATCH OUT FOR WODEN!

Saxons gods were the gods of the north, the same gods as those worshipped by the pagan Germans and later by the Vikings. Greatest of all the northern gods was *Woden*, called *Odin* by the Vikings in later years.

Woden was dangerous. He wandered the world in disguise collecting the souls of warriors slain in battle. He stirred up trouble between people because more battles meant more dead warriors. He needed their souls to fight beside him in a great battle which would take place at the end of the world, a battle between the gods and the forces of darkness in which both the gods and their enemies would all die.

Woden tended to be worshipped by warriors, but *Thunor*, called *Thor* by the Vikings, was popular among churls. He was a huge red-haired god who carried a hammer and made thunder. He was more trustworthy than Woden.

AND WATCH OUT FOR WEDNESBURY!

Only Woden accepted human sacrifices. Sacrificial victims might be first strangled, then thrown into bogs or lakes. Others were hung from trees in 'sacred groves'. Many places in England were centres of Woden worship: watch out for names like *Wednesfield* or 'Woden's Field' and *Wednesbury*, meaning 'Woden's fortress'.

But if you live in one of these places, there's no need for any human sacrifices!

URGSPLFF!!

PAGAN PLACES

Many of us live near pagan shrines and sanctuaries. Mostly Saxons worshipped their gods outdoors by sacred trees, springs or boundaries, although sometimes they built temples which seem to have looked a bit like large farmhouses. *Wih* or *weoh* meant an idol or shrine: does your town or village have a name like *'Weedon'* or *'Wheeley'*?

HEARH HEARH

Or does it sound a bit like someone clearing their throat? *'Hearh'* meant a 'sacred place on a hill'. Names like *Harrow* come from it. In fact Harrow was the largest centre of pagan worship in the country. Much blood must have flowed from the sacrifices at Harrow.

CUTHWULF'S CALENDAR

There was a whole year of god worship and sacrificing for Saxons to get through, starting on 25 December which was the pagan New Year. Take these three Saxon months:

Halgmonath
Month of offerings,
or 'holy month'.

Blotmonath
Month of blood or
sacrifice, when
animals were
slaughtered before
winter.

Solomonath
During the second
month, known as
the 'month of
cakes', cakes were
offered to the
gods.

Not all the months
were for the gods:
During *Thrimilci*
cows were 'milked
three times' a day.
Weodmonath was the
month of weeds.

FANCY SOME CHOCOLATE?

Do you like eating chocolate Easter eggs and Easter bunnies? Nowadays Easter is a Christian festival celebrating Christ's return from the dead after his crucifixion - but it has another history.

Eostre, where the word 'Easter' comes from, was the Saxon goddess of spring and the dawn. The hare was her sacred beast, which is where 'Easter' bunnies come from and Saxon tradition said that the hare was the bringer of eggs during the 'Eostre' festival. Put that in silver paper and eat it!

OH MY GOD!

We still honour the pagan Saxon gods - almost every time we say the name of a day of the week.

> *Sunday* - the day of the Sun
> *Monday* - the day of the Moon
> *Tuesday* - the day of Tiw, god of war
> *Wednesday* - the day of Woden
> *Thursday* - the day of Thunor
> *Friday* - the day of Frig, goddess and wife of Woden
> *Saturday* - all right, so this one isn't Saxon, but it's still sacred to a god - Saturn, the Roman god of agriculture!

There were gods and magic monsters everywhere. There were the elves who caused illnesses, and two types of giant, the *ents* who built great buildings and *thyrs*, who were - just giants.

Also there were dragons which guarded the treasure in old burial mounds and monsters which lived in wild, desolate places. Do you know anyone who looks like this? If so, perhaps they're descended from a Saxon monster ...

'great head, long neck, thin face, horse teeth, throat vomiting flames, twisted jaw, thick lips, strident voice, pigeon breast, scabby thighs, knotty knees, crooked ankles, splay feet ...'

Pagan Saxon religion was always interesting.

ANGELS AND DEVILS

TAMING THE PAGANS

DO WE HAVE TO?!

Around the year AD 577. A Christian priest walks past the slave market in Rome and sees some fair-haired children up for sale. He asks who they are and is told that they are Angles from Britain. 'These are not Angles,' he says: 'They're angels!'.

THESE ARE NOT ANGLES!

From that day on he nurses the ambition to convert all the Angles and Saxons in Britain to Christianity.

Twenty years later that same monk becomes Pope Gregory I, known as 'the Great'. Now that he's Pope he wants to travel to Britain to convert the Angles, but, being Pope, he has to stay in Rome. So instead he asks a monk called Augustine to go to Britain for him.

AD 597 Augustine sets off from Rome with a group of other monks. His mission: to convert the Angles and the Saxons to Christianity.

The further they travel, the more nervous the monks become at the thought of meeting all those pagan Saxons. Half way across France they send a message back to Gregory, begging him not to make them go on.

Gregory insists that they continue.

Later in AD 597, Augustine lands in Kent.

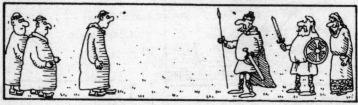

Augustine meets the pagan King Aethelberht of Kent. The king is so afraid of the strangers' magic that he will only meet Augustine out of doors.

Augustine and his monks are allowed to stay in Canterbury and preach to the Saxons.

CUNNING CHRISTIANS

Wherever the missionaries preached they first planted a cross to drive out pagan spirits. But they had to tread carefully and not offend any pagan warriors, who would have been more than happy to slice up the missionaries with their swords.

WOULD YOU MIND AWFULLY IF I ACTUALLY REALLY JUST PREACHED A TINY BIT ABOUT CHRISTIANITY? IF YOU DON'T MIND...

Before the Battle of Chester in 616 Aethelfrith the Ferocious massacred 1,200 monks. They had been praying for the enemy, and as Aethelfrith put it:

'If they pray to their God against us, they too, unarmed as they are, are fighting against us.'

In other words: they had it coming.

The missionaries worked very carefully indeed. First they converted the kings and thegns, then the ordinary people followed. On one occasion ten thousand were converted on a single day! The process of conversion involved being totally dunked in a pond or river so there must have been a lot of wet Saxons sloshing around that day.

Even after large numbers of Saxons had become Christians the missionaries took no chances. They built their churches on pagan sacred sites, following orders from Pope Gregory in a letter from Rome:

'the temples of the idols in that nation [England] ought not to be destroyed, but let the idols that are in them be destroyed ... that the people may resort to the places to which they have been accustomed'.

In this way the Saxons would not feel that their ancient customs were completely lost. And that's why most churches in England are built on pagan sacred sites.

The pagans weren't taking too many chances either - even after they'd been converted! Raedwald, the king of East Anglia whose memorial was probably buried at Sutton Hoo, kept two altars in the same temple - one for Christ, and one at which he offered sacrifices to 'devils'!

PERSUADING THE PAGANS

Compared to Woden and human sacrifice, you might think that Christianity would seem rather too tame to a pagan. Why should any self-respecting Woden-worshipper want to change his or her religion?

Well they did. Edwin, king of Northumbria from 617 - 633, was a pagan when he married the Christian daughter of the king of Kent. She brought a missionary called Paulinus with her when she came to Edwin, and Paulinus argued with Edwin and his thegns in Edwin's great hall. After Paulinus had urged

Edwin and his pagan companions to become Christians, an unnamed pagan thegn described the hopelessness of human life. This is a shortened version of what he said:

> *The life of man, O king, seems to me like the flight of a sparrow through the room where you sit, flying in at one door and out at another. It appears for a short space, but of what went before or what is to follow, we are utterly ignorant. If this new doctrine contains something more certain, it deserves to be followed.*

In other words: Christianity seemed to offer the hope of life after death - and Paulinus sounded so convincing!

Paulinus converted the Northumbrians lock, stock and barrel. Pagan priests were not allowed to carry weapons or ride stallions, but Coifi, Edwin's pagan priest, borrowed weapons, jumped on a stallion, and rode thirty-two kilometres to the pagan shrine at Goodmanham. In front of a crowd which thought he was crazy he threw a spear into the shrine and called on his companions to burn it down! Which they did.

A PAUSE FOR PENDA, THE 'LAST OF THE PAGANS'

Christianity spread fast, but some pagans were prepared to resist it. Some were even prepared to make friends with Christians in order to fight Christianity!

AD 626. A year before Edwin is baptized in the city of York, a ruthless war-leader called Penda is chosen to be king of the Mercians who live in the Midlands. Penda will rule for thirty bloody years.

AD 632. Penda and the Christian British king Caedwalla of North Wales join forces and march on Saxon Northumbria in an unholy combination of wild pagans and Christians.

Later in 632. Edwin is killed by Penda and Caedwalla at the battle of Haethfield. The plain of Haethfield 'reeks with human blood'.

Caedwalla is a Christian but with the heart of a pagan. He is filled with hatred of the Saxons and intends to drive them from England. He shows no mercy to man, woman or child in Northumbria.

Because of Caedwalla and Penda the Northumbrians went back to being pagans for many years. Christianity spread fast, but the old gods didn't give up without a struggle.

WE'RE STILL AROUND!

BRITISH BELIEVERS

... AND THEIR MONKEY BUSINESS

NORTHERN DISCOMFORTS

Even during the darkest days at the end of the Roman Empire, Christianity had survived in England - but only just. It had clung on like a man hanging from a window-sill by his fingertips - and pagan Saxons had behaved like someone trying to stamp on his fingers! Around the edges of England - in Wales, Scotland, Cornwall and Ireland - it was Celtic Britons who had kept the flame of Christianity alive.

You just can't keep a good religion down! Paganism was caught in a pincer movement. To the south Augustine's missionaries argued them into submission, and in the north and west there were a few brave Celtic Christians to do the same ...

During the Saxon period Cornwall was inhabited by British Celts and so was not part of England.

The Celtic Christianity of the Britons was different from the Roman Christianity of Augustine. Celtic monks lived in small, individual cells . They believed in poverty and loneliness and often wandered off into the wide blue yonder, *'going into exile for the love of God, it mattered not whither'*. Later they reached Iceland and there were even tales that a Celtic monk called Brendan sailed as far as America in a small boat, searching for solitude.

ROCK AND SOUL

Off the west coast of Scotland there's a lump of rock about two kilometres long. It's an island, called Iona, and it's incredibly old, older than the beginning of life

---

Their cells were small bare rooms but, unlike prison cells, they often stood alone with their own walls and roof.

on Earth, so old that there are no fossils in it. The Celts believed that Iona had been forged at the beginning of the world and would be the last place to be destroyed on the Day of Doom.

No wonder that Celtic monks built a monastery there.

It was on the Celtic island of Iona that Oswald, the next great Saxon king of Northumbria after Edwin, was educated.

After he had become king of Northumbria, Oswald asked the Celtic monks of Iona to send missionaries to Northumbria. The Celts sent a bishop called Aidan. Aidan didn't like Saxons and he couldn't speak the language, but he went anyway and in 635 founded a monastery on the island of Lindisfarne just off the coast of Northumbria.

Lindisfarne was run in the Celtic style. The monks had little cells and lived lives of poverty. Any money they received from the rich they immediately gave to the poor. They also celebrated Easter on a different day to everyone else, which may not seem very important nowadays - but it was then.

ANOTHER PAUSE FOR PENDA

So now the *Saxon* Northumbrians had become *Celtic* Christians. They had their own little rocky monastery, Lindisfarne, just like rocky Celtic Iona. In fact they might have stayed Celtic Christians for ever, except for one problem. This problem had a capital P and that P stood for ...

Yes, Penda the Pagan was still around. He aimed to make himself Bretwalda of all England, and he wasn't about to let any measly northern Christians stand in his way. He'd bumped off Edwin and now it was Oswald's turn. In a great battle, probably near Oswestry in Shropshire, Penda killed Oswald. Oswald's head and limbs were stuck up on stakes as battle-trophies (there's more about Oswald's head and limbs later).

The town name *Oswestry* may come from 'Oswald's Tree', meaning the place where Oswald raised his standard.

O. BROS. - A SHORT INTERVAL

Saxon names within a family often started with the same letter. Oswald's brother, who followed him shortly after as king of Northumbria was called Oswy. Some of the 'Oses' in the picture below were pagan and some were Christian, but they were all members of the Northumbrian royal family. Can you pick out the pagans? (Answer upside down).

Answer:

You can't tell the Christian from the pagans in this picture. Christian Saxons could be just as warlike as pagan Saxons.

LITTLE THINGS AND BIG THINGS

People in different periods of history have different ways of looking at the world.

Little things: in the modern world, chopping someone's head off with a sword is considered quite a big thing. Among the Anglo-Saxons it was a quite little thing because it happened all the time.

Big things: in the modern world, the date when we have our Easter holiday is quite a little thing - at least compared to murdering people. Among the Anglo-Saxons the date of Easter was a very big thing indeed.

In 642 Oswy was king of Northumbria. He was a Christian like his late lamented brother Oswald. There was only one cloud on his horizon. Oswy was married to a West Saxon princess who followed the Roman system of Christianity and not the Celtic system as Oswy did: this meant (shock horror) that husband and wife celebrated Easter on different days, because of the different ways that the Celtic and Roman churches worked out when Easter should be .

Something had to be done.

He celebrated Easter on 14 April and she celebrated it on 21 April that year.

Oswy called a grand meeting of Roman and Celtic Christians. It was held at Whitby in Yorkshire in 664 and has been known ever since as the 'Synod of Whitby'. There were two matters to clear up:

1   Haircuts
2   The date of Easter

The tonsure was a way of cutting the hair of priests. Celtic Christians shaved the front half of their heads; Roman Christians like Augustine shaved a circular patch in the middle. How to wear your tonsure was a serious question in those days, but the question of the date of Easter was even more important.

The Roman Christians, led by an angry abbot called Wilfred, pointed out that all other Christians in the world agreed with them about Easter, and only the Celtic church disagreed. The poor old Celts who had been busy living in poverty and looking after the poor were no match for Wilfrid's silver tongue.

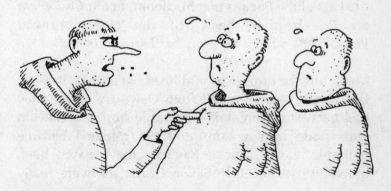

A *synod* is a meeting of important churchmen.

King Oswy asked Wilfrid if the Roman church was founded by Saint Peter 'the keeper of the keys to heaven'. Wilfrid said it was. Oswy then decided that since the Roman church was founded by Saint Peter, he had better follow Peter rather than the Celtic church if he wanted to get into heaven when he died (Oswy is reported to have spoken with a smile).

So the Celtic Christians lost the argument - but they kept their haircuts for a while longer.

YOUNG, HANDSOME CHRISTIAN CHOPS UP GRIZZLED, OLD PAGAN

Christians were popping up everywhere. Even Penda the Last of the Pagans met his doom. In 651 Oswy 'cut off the heathen head' of the eighty-year-old Penda after a two-day battle near Leeds.

Meantime the arms, legs and head of Oswald, Penda's last victim, were rescued from Oswestry where they had been stuck on stakes as battle-trophies. Oswald was made into a saint and his remains became valuable holy relics. Pagans may have been bloodthirsty, but early Saxon Christians were really

At eighty Penda must have been one of the oldest men in England - not bad for a man who had spent most of his life on the warpath.

weird. Take this description of Oswald's head, which was kept at Durham cathedral:

'The roundness of the head, completely spherical, gives off a wonderfully sweet fragrance ... glowing a deep yellow colour which surpasses the yellowness of wax and is closer in its great beauty and loveliness to the appearance of gold ...'

Yes, Christianity had come to the Saxons. Even Penda's son Peada became a Christian.

MORE MONKEY BUSINESS

So maybe you're the right type to be a savage Saxon - but could you have been a glad-to-be-good Saxon? Let's find out - part 1.

I. HOW DID CELTIC MONKS LIKE TO LIVE?

a. In huge monasteries and all crammed into large dormitories at night

b. As far away from people as possible

c. In large libraries with their bunks laid out between the shelves

2. WHAT WAS THE CELTIC TONSURE?

a. A hair style where the front half of the head was shaved

b. A hair style where a round patch on top of the head was shaved

c. A horrible form of scalping reserved for pagans

3. WHAT WAS THE SYNOD OF WHITBY?

a. A meeting of churchmen to decide on the date of Christmas

b. A meeting of churchmen to decide on the date of Easter

Answers on page 121

WISE WOMEN

AND MAD MISSIONARIES
BUT FIRST - SOME *WILD* WOMEN

England had changed. It had thrown away its dirty Dark Age rags and stepped into the satiny silks of civilization (well, not that silky, more woolly and leathery really). Civilization in Europe meant Christianity in those days. In England it was only in Christian cathedrals and monasteries that books were written and ideas were argued over. And right at the front of the writing and arguing were a number of amazing women.

Actually Saxon women, right from the time when they lived in Germany, before they came to England, had always been amazing. Who else except the Germans and Saxons ever called their little girls names like:

Gertrude means 'Spear-Strength'
Hilda means 'Battle Maid'
Griselda means 'Grey Battle Maid'

These were the women whom the Roman writer Tacitus describes as standing behind their men in battle and killing any who fled from the enemy!

But now they turned their talents to doing good.

NUNKS

Question: what do you get when you mix monks with nuns?

Wrong answer: nunks.

Right answer: a double monastery for both monks and nuns. Some were started by rich families as a way to avoid tax (the church didn't have to pay taxes). Many more were started by rich royal women. The very first was a member of the Northumbrian royal family called Hilda. She started the double monastery at Whitby where the famous 'Synod' about haircuts and Easter was held.

Usually the men and women in a double monastery lived totally separate lives. (The Abbess of Wimbourne only gave orders to her monks through a window.) But every now and then things broke down:

The nuns of Coldingham spent their time sewing robes to make themselves look nice - or to give to the men. The nuns and monks had to be separated.

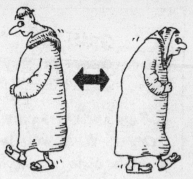

The nuns at Barking had to be warned against satin undergarments, hair arranged with curling irons and jewellery.

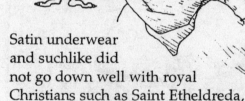

Satin underwear and suchlike did not go down well with royal Christians such as Saint Etheldreda, Abbess of Ely. She didn't even bathe unless she had to!

Bathing does not seem to have been very popular with saints. Saint Cuthbert used to keep his shoes on from one Easter to the next, only taking them off once a year on Maundy Thursday, the Thursday before Easter, for a ritual foot-washing session!

GRISELDA GETS MAD!

*Check it out - are you the right type
to be a seriously savage Saxon?*
Part 4

I. THIS ANCIENT SAXON WOMAN HAS LOST HER TEMPER. WHAT WOULD YOU DO TO STOP HER?

a. Stand up to her and tell her to calm down

b. Keep out of her way

c. Say 'there, there' and try to pat her on the head

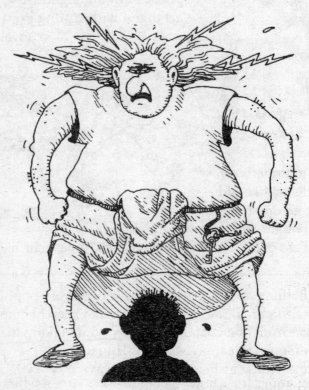

Answer on page 121

WOMEN'S WORK

Of course most women never became nuns and never lived in monasteries. If they hadn't got married and had children the Saxons would have died out and we wouldn't be speaking English today! In fact most English people wouldn't exist at all.

Although the position of Saxon women was nothing like as equal to men as the position of modern women, they still had more freedom than most women of that time. They could own land and make oaths of accusation in court. Also, women ruled inside the home.

They carried the keys to the household and managed any household servants or slaves. They were especially famous for their embroidery, which was the best in all Europe.

PROFS IN PAIRS

Women ran many monasteries, but monks probably outnumbered nuns.

Most monasteries had schools: the oldest school in England is the King's School in Canterbury, which was started by Augustine. Boys as young as three went to live in monasteries, according to Bede, so that the monastic schools could teach them to read and write. Soon Saxon scholars were among the most learned in Northern Europe. Saxon missionaries, including many women, started to travel to the continent of Europe instead of the other way around.

Most of these English missionaries were Northumbrians. Take the two *Willies*:

Willibrord converted savage pagans back in Frisia, where the Saxons had come from in the first place.

Willibald became a bishop in Germany, then travelled even further, to Rome and then on to Syria and lands controlled by the Muslims.

Missionary work could be dangerous. In 754 Saint Boniface, an English missionary to Frisia was massacred by a pagan band while quietly reading in his tent, along with fifty followers. Many of his fellow missionaries were probably women.

Back home the two bold *Alds* had a big impact:

Aldfrith was a son of Oswy. He was the first Saxon king to be more of a scholar than a warrior. Under his rule, Northumbria became a major centre of learning.

Aldhelm was a friend of Aldfrith. He was incredibly clever - so clever that practically no one can understand his writing! He liked to use as many difficult old-fashioned words as possible.

And we have to mention the two brilliant *Bs*:

Benedict Biscop collected books from all over Europe. He built up a big library in Jarrow near Wearmouth. In the Dark Ages books were more precious than gold.

Bede (Venerable) we've met before. He used Biscop's library to write his history of the Angles and Saxons.

Finally (he's not a pair of scholars, but he was worth a pair), there was *Alcuin*. Alcuin was one of Willibrord's relations. He started out as a humble scholar at York but ended up as a chief advisor to the Emperor Charlemagne in Europe.

The descendants of pagan warriors had become the favourite scholars of kings and emperors. Their monasteries were wealthy and paid no taxes.

It was all too good to be true ...

STRIKING VIKINGS

Oh no! The barbarians are back!

Been there, done that

In AD 793 a band of pagan raiders appeared out of the blue off the coast of Northumbria. They landed on the holy island of Lindisfarne and ransacked its monastery, the same monastery that had been founded by the Celtic Bishop Aidan over a hundred and fifty years before.

LOADSA LOOT!

The raiders came in three open boats, about thirty warriors to a boat ...
... remind you of anyone?

The raid on Lindisfarne in 793 was the first Viking attack on England. It took place more than three hundred years after the first Saxons raids on Britain, and the Saxons were completely unprepared for it. But if Hengist or Horsa or any other of the early Saxons had come back from the grave to watch those first Viking raiders, they might well have joined in!

Pagan Vikings and pagan Saxons were as alike as peas in the pod, even though the Viking attacks took place many years after those of the Saxons.

 They both came from Northern Europe, although the Vikings came from a little further north, in Scandinavia.

 They both believed in the same gods. What the Saxons had called *Woden*, the Vikings called *Odin*, and what the Saxons had called *Thunor*, the Vikings called *Thor*. Odin of the Vikings still gathered the souls of warriors slain in battle, and Thor was still the god of thunder.

Considering how the Saxons had behaved when they first came to England, they scarcely had a leg to stand on. But they complained bitterly about the Vikings. As Bishop Alcuin put it:

'Lo, it is nearly 350 years that we and our fathers have inhabited this most lovely land and never before has such a terror appeared in Britain as we have now suffered from this pagan race.'

Above all both pagan Saxons and pagan Vikings loved war. When Viking warriors feasted in the halls of their chiefs, their shields and swords were hung up behind them, ready for battle at a moment's notice - just like the Saxon warriors of long ago.

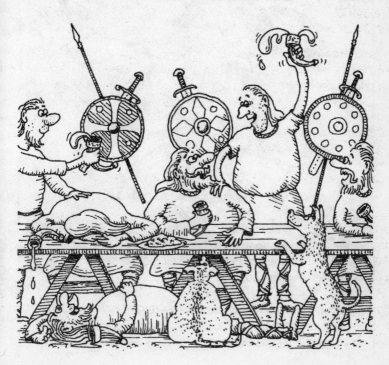

VICIOUS VIKINGS V. SURLY SAXONS

Who were more ruthless - pagan Saxons or pagan Vikings?

Answer

The early Saxons may have been even more ruthless than the Vikings. They seem to have gone in for more human sacrifice for instance. But no one really knows.

GRAB IT AND SCARPER

Vikings were to Saxons what a wasp is to a jammy finger, and what Saxons once were to Britons: they could move in quickly, cause maximum pain, and then buzz off before getting swatted. In other words: they came by sea, they struck where they wanted to, and then, while the poor old Saxons were getting ready to fight back, the Vikings would scarper with the loot.

Also, Viking ships were better than Saxon ships and Vikings were even better sailors. Their ships had sails but were still shallow enough to row far inland up rivers. Nowhere was safe in a narrow country with a long coastline like England.

Nowhere was safe, but monasteries were the least safe of all. There was loads of loot in Saxon monasteries and monks were men of peace who didn't carry weapons. Monasteries were easy pickings and Vikings went for them - like wasps for jam!

QUICKLY BROTHERS

Even if a monastery or town wasn't near water, it might still be in danger of a Viking hit and run attack. Unlike the early Saxons, the Vikings made good use of horses. Sometimes they brought them with them and sometimes they rustled them on arrival. Either way, Viking war bands could travel almost as fast overland as they did by water, although they always dismounted before an attack and fought their battles on foot.

THE FIRST STOP-OVER

The early Viking raids were made by small bands of Norwegian Vikings who took what they could then cleared off back to Norway. The Saxon thegns had some success in fighting them off. They built defensive bridges across rivers - and they buried their money. Several treasure hoards of this period have been dug up, buried by Saxons in times of danger so that the Vikings couldn't get their hands on them. Too bad their owners were often killed before they could dig them up again!

As years went by the Viking raids grew bigger and the Danish Vikings joined in. In AD 850 a force of 350 ships stormed London and then Canterbury. They then decided to stop over for the winter to count their money - and to get ready for the following year. They made their winter camp on the Isle of Thanet in Kent.

This was the start of a new type of Viking warfare.

COME ON OVER!

Now Saxon England was on its knees and there was no time to recover before the fighting season started again in the spring. In 865 a 'great heathen host' led by three ruthless chiefs, Ubbe, Halfdan and Ivar the Boneless defeated King Ella of Northumbria and threw him into a pit where he was bitten to death by snakes. There was now a Viking kingdom in the north of England with its capital city at York.

England, let's face it, is a much nicer country than either Norway or Denmark. Among other things, the climate is warmer and the land is more fertile. The Vikings realized that they were on to a good thing.

Behind the Viking armies which ravaged eastern and northern England in the late 800s came another army - of settlers.

As with Saxon settlers of earlier times, it seems that the Vikings did not throw out all the farmers who were already working the land. Instead they set up new farms between the Saxon villages. The Viking settlers soon learned to speak English and before long it would be impossible to tell a Viking from a Saxon, just as it was impossible to tell an English Celt from a Saxon.

But that was for the future ...

OUR ALFRED

EVERYONE NEEDS A HERO

THE STORY SO FAR

AD 870 The 'Great Heathen Host' of the Vikings has moved south to Reading in the Saxon kingdom of Wessex, plundering and looting as it goes.

Aethelred King of Wessex and his younger brother Alfred lead their army against the Vikings in a series of battles, but fail to drive them from the kingdom.

AD 871 Aethelred dies and Alfred is chosen to be his successor. Alfred is just twenty-two or twenty-three years old. He will become the only English king ever to be called Great.

The Viking army moves north into the kingdom of Mercia then settles down for the winter in London.

The Vikings have become an experienced army and the Saxons are powerless against them. For the next seven years Vikings ravage the land like a swarm of locusts.

MAGNIFICENT MERCIANS

The kingdom of the *Mierce* or 'Boundary Folk' spread like a great big blob across the middle of England. Soon it would join with Wessex under Alfred's leadership to make an even bigger blob.

Mercian kings were descended from an ancient German over-king ➤ 'the best of all mankind between the seas' who must have ruled both Angles and Saxons before they sailed to Britain. For this reason the Mercian royal family seems to have been more 'royal' than other Saxon royal families.

Magnificent Mercian No. 1 Under *Penda the Pagan* (577? - 655), Mercia became the most powerful kingdom in England.

Magnificent Mercian No. 2 Around 774 Offa became the most powerful king in England. He is famous for building *Offa's Dyke*, an earthwork which stretches for about a hundred kilometres right up the border between England and Wales. It was meant to keep out the Welsh.

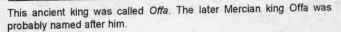

This ancient king was called *Offa*. The later Mercian king Offa was probably named after him.

BACK TO ALFRED

Half of Mercia had been totally ravaged by the great Viking army in 878. It became a Viking province. Meanwhile young Alfred had to hide in the Somerset marshes.

But Alfred fought back against the Vikings and won. Here's what he won:

 Guthrum, leader of the Viking army, was forced to convert to Christianity. Alfred was his godfather.

 The Vikings agreed to stay within the boundaries of 'Danelaw', the land under their control in the east of England.

 The Mercians accepted Alfred's leadership. In fact all English people not ruled by the Vikings submitted to him. They submitted willingly because they saw that Alfred was the best person to lead them against their common Viking enemy. England was starting to become a single country.

GREAT NEWS!

Take a look at these cuttings from the Saxon Klaxon and find out why Alfred was called 'great'.

MONSTER SHIPS!

Alfred has built the first English navy. His ships are larger than Viking ships and are expected to slaughter them if they get the chance.

BURGH BUILDING RECORDS SMASHED!

Walled towns or 'burghs' are being built at record rate. It is planned that no one in the kingdom will be more than fifteen kilometres from their nearest 'burgh' for refuge in case of attack by Viking marauders. Town walls are to be manned by one man from each hide of country round about and that should mean about one man every five metres of wall.

THEGNS TO SCHOOL!

Alfred has decreed that all his top noblemen must learn to read and write English. He hopes that in time all free Englishmen will be able to read.

ANGLO-SAXON CHRONICLE STARTED

Alfred has ordered the history of the Saxons to be written down in English, under the control of his Welsh friend, Bishop Asser.

 The names of many of these towns, such as *Shrewsbury*, end in 'bury'.

ARMY SPLIT IN HALF!

The two halves of our army are to take it in turns to fight or to stay at home and do the farming. In this way it is reckoned that our forces will always be ready to fight off the Vikings and the crops will still be harvested - without our soldiers slinking off home in the middle of a war.

FORBIDDEN BRACELETS

Alfred has ordered golden bracelets be hung at some crossroads as a proof of the peace in his land and to show that in all his kingdom no one will steal them.

BAD MONK, GOOD MONK

Alfred was not just a mighty war leader. He had twice been taken to Rome when he was a child and had seen what civilization could be like at that time. He longed to be able to read books and write them. He asked a Saxon monk called John to help him reintroduce scholarship to England, but John was so severe in his religious beliefs that his fellow monks nearly killed him. John had to go.

Next Alfred asked the Welsh scholar Asser to come and help him. Asser didn't want to leave Wales and live among Saxons, but he agreed to come if he was allowed to spend six months of each year back home. Asser and Alfred soon became good friends and Asser taught Alfred to read and write Latin.

THREE STRONG KINGS

Alfred, his son *Edward* and his grandson *Athelstan* were three of the most powerful Saxon kings that ever ruled in England.

First the sad news: Alfred died in 899. All English people mourned.

Then the glad news: Alfred's successors kept up his good work. His son Edward was recognized as over-king by most of the rulers in Britain, and by 927 Athelstan, his grandson, had captured the Viking city of York.

For the first time the England of both Vikings and Saxons was united under a single ruler. It was during this time that the system of 'shire' counties was started. It looked like England was in for a golden age.

FAT HOPE!

SAXONS  STUFFED!

ALL GOOD THINGS COME TO AN END

TO START WITH - A REALLY BAD KING

Aethelred the Unready 🐟 (978 - 1016) ruled England for nearly forty disastrous years, and during that time he ruined most of the things Alfred had built up.

It started with a murder. In 978 Aethelred's half-brother was murdered by Aethelred's followers. Aethelred was too young to be blamed for the murder, but it was a bad beginning to his reign.

It went on to a massacre. Vikings could smell weakness. They soon knew that Aethelred was a feeble king and they started raiding again. By 1002 they had been at it for twenty years. In desperation and anger Aethelred ordered the

---

The name *'Aethelred the Unready'* was originally *'Aethelred Unraed'*, meaning 'Aethelred No-council' or 'badly-advised'.

killing of all Danes then living in England. The sister of King Swein Forkbeard of Denmark was in England at the time. They killed her too - which wasn't very clever.

It continued with a mistake. Aethelred married as his second wife Emma, sister of Duke Richard of Normandy (more on that later).

And it ended with a disaster. In 1009 an army of King Swein Forkbeard of Denmark conquered England, partly to revenge the death of his sister. Aethelred fled abroad and the

rest of his life was spent in desperate attempts to recover his kingdom.

THE PRICE OF PEACE ...

When Aethelred came to the throne, England was a wealthy nation. English coins were the best in Europe.

penig (penny)

sceat

styca

Dane was what the English called Vikings at this time.

The Vikings came to realize that they didn't need to bother with looting and pillaging. All they had to do was threaten it. Then, if they were lucky the Saxons would pay them to go away!

The first payment of *Danegeld* as it was called was made in 868. Surprise, surprise, it had the opposite effect to what was intended - the Vikings came back for more - and more - and more. For the Vikings, Danegeld was like pocket money with no limits on it.

Strong kings like Alfred refused to pay it, but weak kings such as Aethelred saw Danegeld as an easy way to avoid trouble. Aethlered paid out massive sums of money to the Danes. They bled the country dry. More Saxon coins have been found in Scandinavia than have been found in England.

DANEFUL PAINS - AND NOT SO PAINFUL DANES

The Danes had been a pain for years. Looting and pillaging is not a way to get yourself liked. But they became Christians. And once Swein Forkbeard had defeated Aethelred, they were kings of all England - and things started to change.

1. Swein Forkbeard
- a bit of a Viking

2. Swein's son Cnut - a good king. The English liked him.

3. Harthacnut - Cnut's son, both good and bad

Harthacnut died while drinking in 1041. He was the last of the three Danish kings of England. After his death Edward (later known as 'The Confessor') was chosen to be king. Edward's stepfather had been King Cnut, but Edward was a Saxon - his real father was Aethelred the Unready. Anything to do with Aethelred was bad news for England - and Edward was really no exception.

NORMAL NORMANS

In 911 a huge Viking called Rollo knelt to kiss the foot of Charles the Simple, King of France, as an act of homage. The king had just given him lands in what is now Normandy as part of a peace treaty. Except that Rollo didn't kneel, he pulled the king's foot up to his mouth thus making the king fall over backwards. How Rollo's Viking friends laughed - typical!

OOPS! SORRY!

Despite his rude behaviour Rollo became the first Duke of Normandy, and that's why Normandy is called what it is, after the 'nor(th)men' who were given it. The Normans started off as bullies, and that's how they stayed - as the Saxons were soon to discover ...

AND GRUMPY SAXONS

Edward the Confessor liked Normans. He spent his youth in Normandy because his mother Emma was a Norman, and he filled his court in London with Norman friends after he came to the throne.

Possibly the same person as a Viking known as *Hrolf the Ganger*, or 'Walker', so called because he was so big no horse could carry him.

In 1052 the Duke of Normandy himself, a red-haired man called William, visited Edward the Confessor in London. It seems that during this visit Edward promised the crown of England to William - and changed the course of English history.

Edward invited more and more Normans to join him in England. It seemed to many Saxons that the Normans were taking over. The Saxon lords became fed up and grumpy. The grumpiest were led by a powerful earl called Harold Godwine.

Then on 5 January 1066 Edward died. His council were in an anti-French mood. They decided Harold Godwine was the right man to be the next king of England.

William Duke of Normandy did not agree ...

THE END

Harold scarcely had time to slip the crown of England on his head. By September he was being squeezed in the middle of a horrible sandwich. To the north, an army of Norwegian Vikings had already landed. To the south, an army of Normans led by William the Duke was just about to land.

Harold rushed north and defeated the Norwegians at a place called Stamford Bridge. Then he rushed south again to beat off the Normans, who were waiting for him at Hastings in Sussex. William's Norman army was smaller than Harold's, but they hadn't just fought an army of Norwegians and they hadn't just marched south at top speed for three hundred kilometres. The Normans were ready for a fight, but the Saxons could have done with a rest.

The Saxon and Norman armies met on the morning of 14 October on the road to Hastings. Not so very far from the beach in Kent where Hengist and Horsa had landed in AD 449 all that long time ago. To start with, the two-handed Saxon battleaxes sliced through the armour of the Norman knights, but slowly the Normans gained the upper hand. Harold and his companions fought bravely all day, but finally Harold was killed by a chance Norman arrow and Saxon resistance started to crumble.

In fact the Saxon shield-wall held firm till almost the end. Every time a warrior fell the other warriors drew closer to cover the space where the fallen man had stood, until the shield-wall was little more than a ragged line.

Saxon England came to an end that day, but Hengist and Horsa, those fierce warriors, would have been proud of the warriors who fought and died at Hastings.

ARE YOU AN ANGLE OR A SAXON?

- OR A NORMAN OR A CELT?

SAXONS SUMMED UP

William Duke of Normandy, soon to be known as 'William the Conqueror', lost no time in seizing control of the rest of England. Within a few years the whole of Saxon England was being ruled by Frenchmen, and the Saxon Age had come to an end. The Middle Ages was about to begin.

But life goes on. William had won a rich prize and he had no wish to disturb or destroy it. He chose to rule by the laws and customs of the Saxons. Because of this we owe far more to the Saxons than we do to the Normans who defeated them.

> ### THINGS WE HAVE INHERITED FROM THE SAXONS
>
> the words 'England' and 'English'
> the English language
> the days of the week
> the English system of law
> most English towns and villages
> most English counties
> - in fact almost everything English

Throughout history waves of newcomers have arrived on the islands of Britain. There was a time when the Celts were new, even before the Saxons came along. Each new wave of newcomers has mixed and mingled with the people who were there when they arrived.

The Saxons weren't the first newcomers, and they certainly weren't the last, but they changed Britain more than any other group of people before or after them.

SAINTED!

So maybe you're the right type to be a savage Saxon - but could you have been a glad-to-be-good Saxon (or even a saint)? Let's find out - part 2.

1. DO YOU LIKE SMELLY FEET?

a. Not really, but not washing is a good way for a saint to behave
b. They smell disgusting
c. They smell nice - but saints aren't meant to enjoy themselves

2. WHAT'S GOOD ABOUT DOUBLE MONASTERIES?

a. You have to say twice the prayers of a single monastery
b. You get to meet lots of nice monks or nuns of the opposite sex
c. Double monasteries are all right as long as you never meet the opposite sex

3. WHAT'S GOOD ABOUT BEING A SAINT?

a. You go to heaven when you die
b. Nothing - it's really boring
c. You never have to wash and you get to meet lots of interesting people

Answers on next page

ANSWERS

SECTION 1

Are you the right type to be as seriously savage Saxon?
Score 10 points for each correct answer.

Part 1	Part 2	Part 3	Part 4
1 - c	1 - a	1 - c	a
2 - c	2 - c	2 - b	
3 - a	3 - b	3 - a	

SECTION 2

Could you have been a glad-to-be-good Saxon (or even a Saxon saint)?
Score *minus* 10 points for each correct answer.

Part 1	Part 2
1 - b	1 - a
2 - a	2 - c
3 - b	3 - a or b

GRAND TOTAL

*To arrive at your final total, **subtract** points scored in section 2 from points scored in section 1.*

60 to 100	You are seriously savage. Got any long, sharp knives?
30 to 60	Not bad - for a churl. You'll be all right on a war party.
0 to 30	What a wimp! Go back to noddy-land!
-30 to 0	You are seriously good.
-30 to -60	You are disgustingly good - and you stink like a ferret!

INDEX

NOW READ ON

If you want to know more about the Romans in Britain, see if your local library or bookshop has any of these books.

THE WARRIOR KINGS OF SAXON ENGLAND
By Ralph Whitlock (Moonraker Press 1977) If you like a good fight, then this is the book for you! All you need to know about the brave heroes who led the Saxon fight against the Vikings.

NORTHANHYMBRE SAGA
By John Marsden (Kyle Cathie Ltd. 1992) Delve into a depth of detail about the Dark Ages. An excellent introduction to Aethelfrith the Ferocious, Penda the Last of the Pagans and their bloodthirsty mates.

ALFRED THE GREAT
By Ronald Mcnair Scott (The Book Guild Ltd. 1993) Follow the story of England's greatest king from his birth in war-torn Wessex and his time on the run in the Somerset marshes, to his great victories and his friendship with Asser the reluctant Welsh bishop.

THE ANGLO-SAXONS
Edited by James Campbell (Phaidon Press Ltd. 1982) More photographs than you could fit on your bedroom wall! - well almost. Get behind the words (there's lots of them as well) and take a look at the evidence. If you remember half of what's in this book, you'll be an expert on the Saxons.

About the author

Bob Fowke is a well-known author of children's information books. Writing under various pen names and with various friends and colleagues, he has created around fifty unusual and entertaining works on all manner of subjects.

There's always more to Fowke books than meets the eye - so don't be misled by the humorous style (just check out the index at the end of this book!). They're just the thing if you want your brain to bulge and your information banks to burble.

Bob Fowke is the youngest son of a Sussex vicar, and spent his childhood in the large, draughty vicarage of the village of Fletching (where the famous historian Edward Gibbon is buried). After years of travel and adventure, he now lives quietly in Shropshire.

What They Don't Tell You About ...
ORDER FORM

0 340 71330 5	ART	£3.99
0 340 63622 X	QUEEN VICTORIA	£3.99
0 340 63621 1	HENRY VIII	£3.99
0 340 69349 5	LIVING THINGS	£3.99
0 340 63624 6	VILLAINS THROUGH THE AGES	£3.50
0 340 67093 2	SHAKESPEARE	£3.99
0 340 69350 9	STORY OF SCIENCE	£3.99
0 340 65614 X	ANCIENT EGYPTIANS	£3.99
0 340 65613 1	ELIZABETH I	£3.99
0 340 68611 1	VIKINGS	£3.99
0 340 68612 X	WORLD WAR II	£3.99
0 340 70922 7	ROMANS	£3.99
0 340 70921 9	ANGLO SAXONS	£3.99
0 340 71329 1	PLANET EARTH	£3.99
0 340 71328 3	ANCIENT GREEKS	£3.99
0 340 68995 1	STORY OF MUSIC	£3.99
0 340 73611 9	OLYMPICS	£3.99

All Hodder Children's books are available at your local bookshop or newsagent, or can be ordered direct from the publisher. Just write to the address below. Prices and availability subject to change without notice.

Hodder Children's Books, Cash Sales Department, Bookpoint, 39 Milton Park, Abingdon, Oxon, OX14 4TD, UK.
Email address: orders@bookpoint.co.uk

Please enclose a cheque or postal order made payable to Bookpoint Ltd to the value of the cover price and allow the following for postage and packing:
UK & BFPO - £1.00 for the first book, 50p for the second book, and 30p for each additional book ordered, up to a maximum charge of £3.00.
OVERSEAS & EIRE - £2.00 for the first book, £1.00 for the second book, and 50p for each additional book.

If you have a credit card you may order by telephone - (01235) 400414 (lines open 9 am - 6 pm, Monday to Saturday; 24 hour message answering service). Alternatively you can send a fax on 01235 400454.